鳥山 明

On days when I have to ink **Dragon Ball**, I get up around noon, eat breakfast, and then around 1 p.m. I begin working together with my assistant Matsuyama. I take a break from 7 to 8 p.m. to eat dinner, walk my dog, and feed my bird. Matsuyama goes home around 9 p.m. and I continue to work while watching television. I usually take a bath around 11 p.m. and then after that I relax but I continue to do a bit more work. I will then go to sleep around 4 a.m. And that is what my inking days are like.

–Akira Toriyama, 1987

Artist/writer Akira Toriyama burst onto the manga scene in 1980 with the wildly popular **Dr. Slump**, a science fiction comedy about the adventures of a mad scientist and his android "daughter." In 1984 he created his hit series **Dragon Ball**, which ran until 1995 in Shueisha's bestselling magazine **Weekly Shonen Jump**, and was translated into foreign languages around the world. Since **Dragon Ball**, he has worked on a variety of short series, including **Cowa!**, **Kajika**, **Sand Land**, and **Neko Majin**, as well as a children's book, **Toccio the Angel**. He is also known for his design work on video games, particularly the **Dragon Warrior** RPG series. He lives with his family in Japan.

DRAGON BALL VOL. 8
The SHONEN JUMP Manga Edition

This graphic novel is number 8 in a series of 42.

STORY AND ART BY
AKIRA TORIYAMA
ENGLISH ADAPTATION BY
GERARD JONES

Translation/Mari Morimoto
Touch-Up Art & Lettering/Wayne Truman
Cover Design/Sean Lee & Dan Ziegler
Graphics & Design/Sean Lee
Senior Editor/Jason Thompson

Editor in Chief, Books/Alvin Lu
Editor in Chief, Magazines/Marc Weidenbaum
VP of Publishing Licensing/Rika Inouye
VP of Sales/Gonzalo Ferreyra
Sr. VP of Marketing/Liza Coppola
Publisher/Hyoe Narita

Printed in Canada

In the original Japanese edition, DRAGON BALL and DRAGON BALL Z are known collectively as the 42-volume series DRAGON BALL. The English DRAGON BALL Z was originally volumes 17-42 of the Japanese DRAGON BALL.

Published by VIZ Media, LLC
P.O. Box 77010 • San Francisco, CA 94107

SHONEN JUMP Manga Edition
10 9 8 7 6 5 4
First printing, May 2003
Fourth printing, March 2008

www.viz.com

PARENTAL ADVISORY
DRAGON BALL is rated T for Teen. It may contain violence, language, alcohol or tobacco use, or suggestive situations. It is recommended for ages 13 and up.

ratings.viz.com

www.shonenjump.com

SHONEN JUMP MANGA

DRAGON BALL

Vol. 8

DB: 8 of 42

STORY AND ART BY
AKIRA TORIYAMA

THE MAIN CHARACTERS

Son Goku
Monkey-tailed Son Goku has always been stronger than normal. His grandfather Gohan gave him the *nyoibô*, a magic staff, and Kame-Sen'nin gave him the *kinto'un*, a magic flying cloud.

Bulma
A genius inventor, Bulma met Goku on her quest for the seven magical Dragon Balls.

Yamcha
Yamcha used to be a desert bandit, but he went to the city to be Bulma's on-and-off boyfriend. He uses "Fist of the Wolf-Fang" kung-fu. Pu'ar is his shapeshifting friend.

Lunch
A strange woman whose personality changes whenever she sneezes.

Kuririn
Goku's former martial arts schoolmate under Kame-Sen'nin.

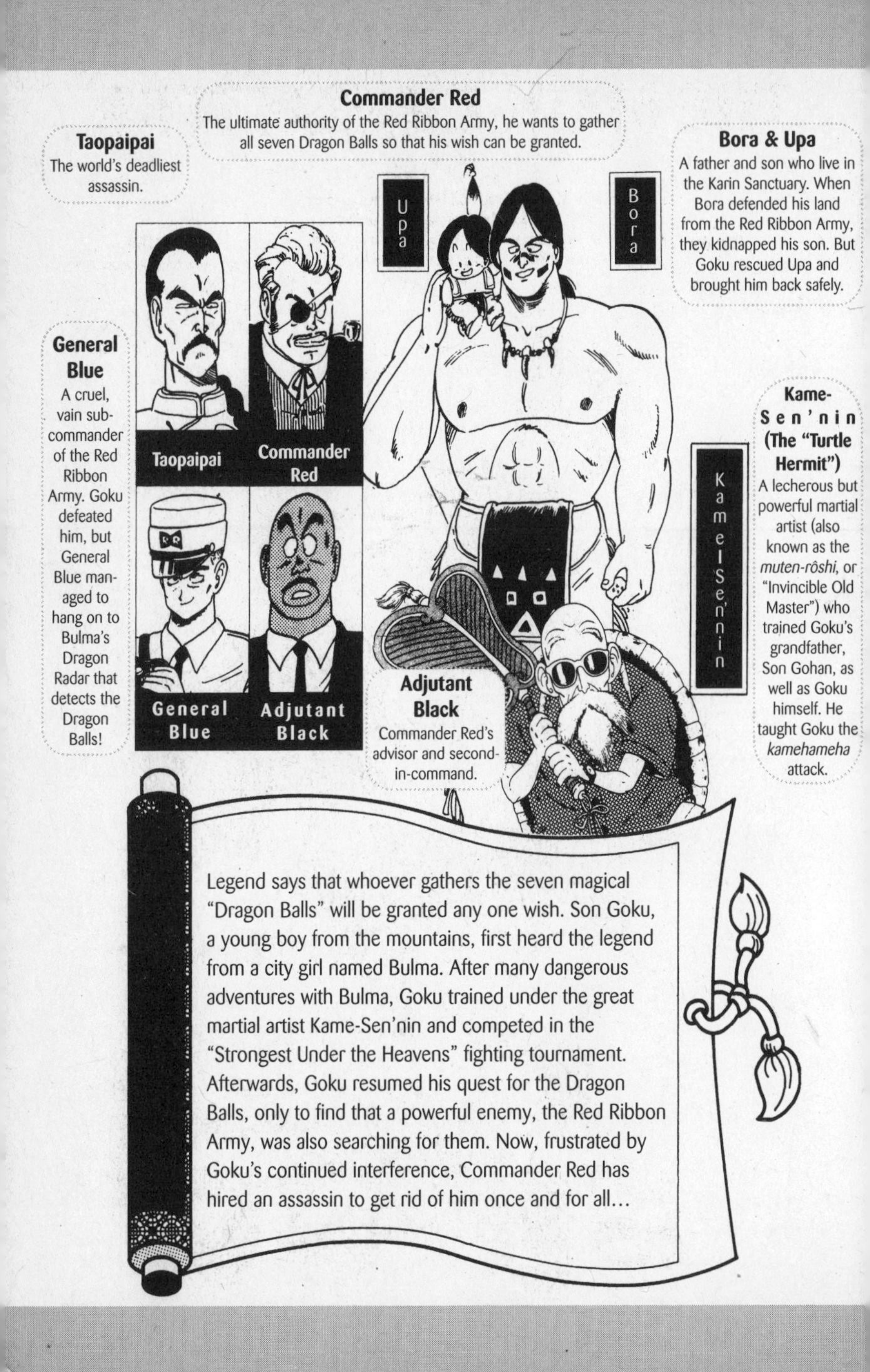

Legend says that whoever gathers the seven magical "Dragon Balls" will be granted any one wish. Son Goku, a young boy from the mountains, first heard the legend from a city girl named Bulma. After many dangerous adventures with Bulma, Goku trained under the great martial artist Kame-Sen'nin and competed in the "Strongest Under the Heavens" fighting tournament. Afterwards, Goku resumed his quest for the Dragon Balls, only to find that a powerful enemy, the Red Ribbon Army, was also searching for them. Now, frustrated by Goku's continued interference, Commander Red has hired an assassin to get rid of him once and for all...

DRAGON BALL 8

Tale 85 • Taopaipai the Assassin

CHEEP
CHEEP
CHEEP
THANK YOU FOR RESCUING MY SON.
IT WAS NOTHIN', JUST PART OF BEATING UP THAT ARMY GUY!
THERE IT IS !!!
MISTER, THAT'S A DRAGON BALL YOU'RE HOLDING IN YOUR HAND!!!

CAN I SEE IT, CAN I SEE IT, PLEASE?!!
DO YOU SEEK THIS SPHERE TOO...?
YAHOO--!!! IT'S GOT FOUR STARS-- !!!
I FOUND GRAMPA'S "SÛSHINCHÛ !!"
WOO-HOO WOO-HOO-- !!!
WHAT IS THIS? WHAT IS THE MEANING OF THAT SPHERE?
RED RIBBON ARMY HQ
SHUUUUN

SKRII
HEY, HEY, HEY!!
WHERE DO YOU THINK YOU ARE, HUH?!!
TAP
SCRAM!! UNLESS YOU WANT TO BE TURNED TO DOG FOOD, THAT IS!!
HO-!!!
FYOOOO
BAM

GNNG
DO YOU MAKE A HABIT OF FORGETTING YOUR SUPERIORS' FACES, WORM!?
G-GENERAL BLUE!! I-- I--
JUST HURRY UP AND OPEN THE GATE!
DOOM
I AM TAOPAIPAI... MASTER ASSASSIN !

GOOD OF YOU TO COME, TAOPAIPAI.
I MUST WARN YOU IN ADVANCE...
...MY SERVICES DO NOT COME CHEAPLY.
IF YOU DO THE JOB WELL, I WILL PAY WHATEVER YOU ASK.
FOR EACH STRIKE... I MUST RECEIVE 100 MILLION ZENII!
KILL YOU!
100 M-MILLION ZENII... ?!!
HOWEVER, YOU'RE IN LUCK. THIS YEAR HAPPENS TO BE MY 20TH ANNIVERSARY HALF-PRICE SALE.
THAT MAKES A VERY REA-SONABLE 50 MILLION ZENII A HEAD...
...
TH-THANK YOU...
YOU'D BETTER BE THE REAL TAOPAIPAI....
WOULD YOU LIKE TO TEST ME?

NOK NOK
O-OH, NO, THAT'S QUITE ALL RIGHT...
WH- WHO IS IT?
IT IS I, BLUE!
GENERAL BLUE, EH...?
ENTER...
REPORTING AS ORDERED, SIR!
I'M AMAZED THAT YOU'VE RETURNED.
WELL, IT WAS QUITE A JOB... STEALING AIRPLANES... CARS... ETC....
THAT'S NOT WHAT I MEANT.
I AM **AMAZED** THAT YOU CAN NONCHALANTLY STROLL BACK IN HERE AFTER LOSING THE DRAGON BALLS TO THAT BRAT SON GOKU!
B-B-BUT... THAT COULDN'T BE HELPED!
A-A-AND I DID GET THE ENEMY'S RADAR !!

LOOK! LOOK! IT CAN ZOOM IN AND OUT AT WILL...
MAKING IT POSSIBLE TO PINPOINT THE DRAGON BALL'S EXACT LOCATION EASILY!
IT'S THAT SMALL...?
WITH THIS, I WILL GATHER ALL SEVEN DRAGON BALLS FOR YOU!!
THAT IS QUITE A USEFUL ACCOMPLISHMENT...
BUT MY ORDER WAS TO BRING BACK THE DRAGON BALLS!
THOSE WHO CANNOT COMPLETE THEIR DUTIES ARE TO BE EXECUTED!
BUT...
GASP
I... I...
HOWEVER. YOU *HAVE* SERVED THE RED RIBBON ARMY VERY WELL IN THE PAST.
I WILL GIVE YOU A CHANCE TO REDEEM YOURSELF. IF YOU FIGHT TAOPAIPAI HERE AND WIN...YOUR HONOR WILL BE RESTORED.
THANK YOU, SIR!

SO...YOU WOULD BE THE TAOPAIPAI THEY CALL "THE WORLD'S GREATEST KILLER," I SUPPOSE...?
DO YOU WANT MY AUTOGRAPH?

SURE. I'D LIKE TO SEE YOUR HANDI-WORK.
I'D LIKE TO RECEIVE A KILL FEE FOR HIM TOO, IF THAT'S ALL RIGHT?
IF YOU'RE THE *WORLD'S* GREATEST, THEN I AM THE *UNIVERSE'S* GREATEST!
OHO HO HO...

I'M LOOKING FORWARD TO IT!
AGAINST A NOVICE LIKE YOU, I WON'T USE MY ARMS OR LEGS... BUT JUST MY *TONGUE* TO TAKE YOU DOWN!
BEGIN!!

HYOH !!!!
VNNN
DODGE!
BMM
SLURP!
BLAAAA!
POIK
ZOK

!!
!!
DMM
HE REALLY IS AS DEADLY AS HE CLAIMS TO BE...
I WOULDN'T EVEN SAY "BLOW"...
H-HE TOOK DOWN BLUE... W-WITH JUST ONE BLOW....
I CRAVE A WORTHY OPPO-NENT...
FEH...
ENOUGH FORMALITIES. SHOW ME WHO MY REAL TARGETS ARE.
NOW.
殺

WHAT-- THAT LITTLE BOY !?
THAT'S WHAT WE KEPT SAYING...AND REGRETTING IT.
WELL, IT'S NO MATTER TO ME. AS LONG AS I RECEIVE MY PAYMENT, I WILL ERASE WHOMEVER YOU WANT.
VERY PROFES-SIONAL.
AND, UH, BY THE WAY... THAT BRAT SON GOKU SHOULD HAVE FOUR BALLS ON HIM... WE'D APPRECIATE IT IF YOU COULD JUST BRING THEM BACK WITH YOU, HM?
THEY LOOK LIKE THIS.
AND IF ANYONE ELSE GETS IN YOUR WAY, FEEL FREE TO KILL THEM, NO MATTER HOW MANY THERE ARE.
I UNDER-STAND. THE LOCATION IS A PLACE CALLED KARIN, ABOUT 2300 KILOMETERS TO THE NORTHEAST, CORRECT ?
WE HAVE A JET PREPARED FOR YOU-- THIS WAY, PLEASE.
THAT WILL NOT BE NECESSARY-- AN AIRPLANE WILL TAKE TOO LONG.
MAY I HAVE THIS ONE PILLAR HERE?
HUH ?
THE PILLAR? WH-WHAT DO YOU MEAN?

HOP
TM
THP
KILL YOU!
TP
BWOK
2300 KILO-METERS, MMM... ?
WELL, THEN, I SHOULD BE BACK IN ABOUT 30 MINUTES...
VNNN
PYOH!!!!

SHHHH!!
HOOOOOSH
TUP
THE KARIN SANCTUARY
WH-WHAT A TERRIBLE FELLOW...
GYAH-HAHA!!! IT'S AS IF WE'VE ALREADY GOT THOSE DRAGON BALLS IN OUR HANDS !!!
AND ALL SEVEN TOGETHER WILL GRANT ANY WISH...?HMM...NO WONDER THEY WERE SO INTENT UPON TAKING THIS SPHERE....

NEXT: Fighting Fire with Fire!

Tale 86
The Devastating Dodon-pa!!!

IT'S COMING THIS WAY!!
LOOK OUT !!!
DOM

ALO~
HA~!
TUP
WH-WHO IN THE WORLD ARE YOU?!!
...
I'M THE WORLD'S GREATEST ASSASSIN....
TAOPAIPAI !
ASSASSIN....
WHAT BUSINESS DOES A KILLER HAVE IN THIS HOLY PLACE?

I HAVE NO BUSINESS WITH THIS PLACE-- I HAVE BUSINESS ONLY WITH THAT LAD OVER THERE.
WHAT ?!
BUSINESS WITH ME?
I DON'T EVEN KNOW YOU, MISTER.
PERHAPS YOU WILL UNDERSTAND IF I TELL YOU THAT I WAS HIRED BY THE RED RIBBON ARMY.
MY ASSIGNMENT IS TO KILL YOU, SINCE YOU ARE INTERFERING WITH THEIR QUEST FOR SOME BALLS.
RED RIBBON-- ?!!
THEM AGAIN!! MAN, THEY ARE *SO* STUBBORN !!
F-FATHER! YOU CAN'T LET THEM DO IT!!
THIS YOUTH SAVED MY SON'S LIFE.
IF YOU WILL NOT LEAVE QUIETLY, **I** WILL STAND AGAINST YOU.

HEY, THAT'S OKAY! HE'S MY ENEMY!
TO DEFEND THE SACRED LAND OF KARIN IS MY SWORN DUTY.
STAY BACK, UPA.
HEH HEH HEH, WHAT A FOOL....
TO DELIBERATELY CHOOSE DEATH...!
NOW COME!!
FATHER, GOOD LUCK--!!
HEH HEH HEH... YOU THINK YOU'RE FAIRLY GOOD, DO YOU?
WELL THEN... I'LL MAKE THE FIRST MOVE WITH-OUT ANY QUALMS.

YO !
OH !!!
VOOO
H-HE'S FAST...!!!!
NGH...!! G-G-GGG... !!!
HRRR... !!
MM? SOMETHING THE MATTER? YOU'RE NOT MOVING AT ALL!
WELL THEN, ALLOW ME TO MOVE YOU...

HWIII
HERE!
!!
HENH.
TUGG
SPOP
WHOA!!!

WOULD YOU LIKE YOUR SPEAR BACK?!!
SHHHH
FATHER-- !!!
FOOEY !!!
KINTO'UN !!!
OH NO !!!!
AARGH !
ZUDD
....!!!
FYOOOO

DM
M

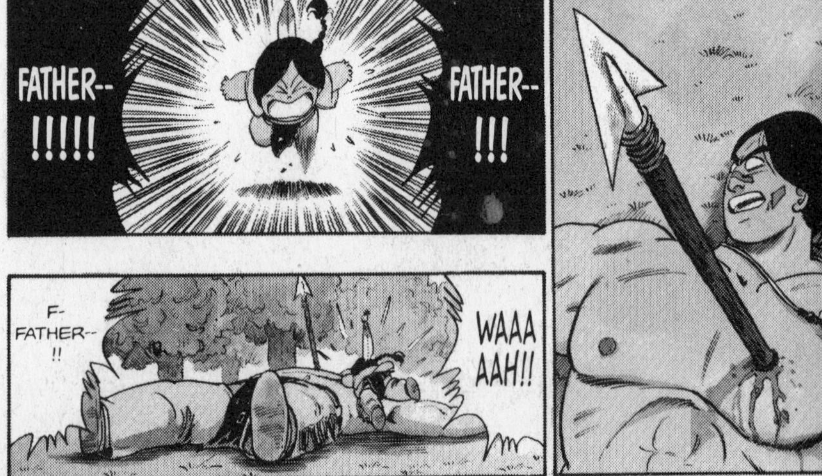
FATHER-- !!!
FATHER-- !!!!!
WAAA AAH!!
F- FATHER-- !!

YOU-- !!!
YOU-- ASSASSIN-- !!!!
VSH
BNG
SHHH

CHK
BAM!
DMP
...
IS THAT ALL? HOW PITIFUL.

I'LL GET YOU-- !!
STAGGER
HO- YOU DIDN'T DIE, EH?
TAKE THIS... !!
KA... ME...
HA... ME...
HAAAAA !!!
BOOM
!!

FWAAAA
YOU...
...YOU RUINED MY CLOTHES... !
PFF
PFFFF
TH-TH-THAT'S ALL ?!?!
DODON'PA!!

NEXT: Goku: R.I.P.?

Tale 87 • The Great Climb
BAMM
THE WORLD'S GREATEST ASSASSIN, TAOPAIPAI, HIRED BY THE RED RIBBON ARMY, HAS KILLED UPA'S FATHER...AND NOW GOKU HIMSELF! NOT ONLY THAT, HE TOOK THE DRAGON BALLS TOO...
I'VE DISPATCHED MY TARGET AND COLLECTED THESE BALLS, PRECISELY AS REQUESTED....
BUT THERE'S NO WAY THE WORLD'S GREATEST ASSASSIN CAN GO HOME LOOKING LIKE THIS! TIME FOR A TRIP TO MY TAILOR....

NOW THEN....
...
YOU...YOU MONSTER...!
YOU KILLED MY FATHER-- AND OUR FRIEND!!
WHIFF
KWIII
PUFF
KONG
!!
YAAA! YAAA!
HA HA HA... DON'T YOU KNOW HOW LUCKY YOU ARE TO BE ALIVE?
YOU SHOULD THANK ME!

VNNN
BOING

TUP

HHHOOO
RED RIBBON ARMY HQ
HEH HEH HEH! LEAVE IT TO TAOPAIPAI!
IT LOOKS LIKE EVERY-THING WENT PERF----

WAIT.
DON'T YOU NOTICE SOMETHING STRANGE....?
WHAT?
THERE ARE SUPPOSED TO BE FOUR BALLS...BUT HE ONLY GRABBED THREE.
1 at The Land of Karin
3 Taopaipai took
1 at Red Ribbon Army HQ
AND WHY ISN'T TAOPAIPAI HEADING STRAIGHT BACK HERE?
WHAT'S THAT MURDERER UP TO....?
EXACTLY AS DRAWN, DO YOU UNDERSTAND? NO MISTAKES.
Y-YES, SIR!

HOW LONG WILL IT TAKE?
IF I HAVE A WEEK, I MAY BE ABLE TO...
YOU HAVE 3 DAYS.
I CAN SUFFER THIS EMBARRAS-SING OUTFIT NO LONGER THAN THAT.
T-THREE DAYS...? BUT....
HAVE YOU NEVER HEARD OF TAOPAIPAI?
HRRR
N-N NO!! I MEAN, Y-Y-YES!! I KNOW WHO YOU ARE!!
THREE DAYS IT'LL BE!!
WHERE'S YOUR PHONE?
R-R-RIGHT OVER HERE, SIR! THANK YOU!
pip pip pip
COMMANDER! WE'VE RECEIVED A CALL FROM MR. TAOPAIPAI!
HMPH!
TAOPAIPAI! WHAT THE HECK'S GOING ON?
WHAT ARE YOU DOING?

I'VE DISPATCHED YOUR ENEMY, SO PLEASE BE SURE MY FEE IS WAITING FOR ME.
I WILL RETURN IN THREE DAYS.
THAT'S ALL FINE AND DANDY, BUT DON'T YOU ONLY HAVE 3 OF THE SUPPOSEDLY 4 DRAGON BALLS YOU WERE GOING TO BRING BACK?!
WHAT...?!
OH-HO... THERE ARE ONLY 3!
MY TARGET MUST HAVE BEEN CARRYING ONE ON HIS PERSON... ALL RIGHT, I'LL RETRIEVE IT BEFORE I RETURN.
IN THAT CASE, TAKE YOUR TIME. AS LONG AS THAT BRAT'S DEAD, THERE SHOULDN'T BE ANY MORE INTERFERENCE. THANKS MUCH, AND WE'LL SEE YOU IN THREE DAYS.
SO THAT'S IT! WE'VE WON!
YOU WERE WISE TO HIRE TAOPAIPAI, SIR.
F-FATHER... IF ONLY I WERE STRONGER...

SNIFF... I'VE GOT TO DIG GOKU'S GRAVE TOO.
ZNCH
SHF
TWIK
N... NNH...
HUH ?!
Y-YOU'RE STILL ALIVE!!
ARE YOU ALL RIGHT?! HANG IN THERE!!
O-OWW...
ROLLL
THE DRAGON BALL !!
IT WAS IN YOUR UNIFORM-- THAT'S WHAT SAVED YOU!!

HUH...
GRAMPA SAVED MY LIFE.....
...
IS THAT YOUR DAD'S GRAVE... ?!
YES... SNIFF....I WISH HE COULD BE STILL ALIVE TOO.......
...
SOBB SOBB
ALL RIGHT !!!
I'LL GATHER ALL THE DRAGON BALLS AND BRING YOUR DAD BACK TO LIFE!!

WHAT?! YOU CAN REALLY DO THAT?!
PROBABLY!! THAT DRAGON GOD IS SUPPOSED TO GIVE YOU ANY WISH !!
...BUT THAT MAN TOOK ALL OF THE BALLS THAT WERE IN YOUR BAG, GOKU...
...HMMM... HE DID, DID HE...
GUESS HE DIDN'T KNOW I WAS CARRYING THIS FOUR-STAR BALL....
WELL, HE'LL PROBABLY COME BACK FOR IT.... AND WHEN HE DOES, I'M GONNA TAKE ALL THE REST BACK FROM HIM...!
HE SURE IS STRONG, THOUGH...
NO WAY I COULD BEAT HIM IN A MATCH... FIRST TIME I'VE EVER RUN INTO SOMEBODY LIKE THAT...
HEY !
GOKU, WHY DON'T YOU TRY CLIMBING THE KARIN TOWER ?!
RIGHT...!! AND AT THE TOP OF THE TOWER THERE'S SUPPOSED TO BE A MEDICINE THAT MAKES YOU STRONGER, HUH!?
I KNOW THERE IS !
HUH ?!
I'LL BET YOU COULD DO IT !!

IT'D BE SO EASY TO USE KINTO'UN, BUT...
YOU HAVE TO CLIMB IT WITHOUT ANY HELP, RIGHT?
UH-HUH.... THE MASTER OF THE TOWER MAKES SURE....
O-KAY!! I'M GONNA TRY IT!
PLEASE DON'T FALL, GOKU!
THAT GUY'LL PROBABLY BE COMING BACK TO TAKE THIS DRAGON BALL....
SO YOU BETTER GO HIDE SOME-WHERE, OK?
OK!
ALL RIGHT, I'M ON MY WAY!
GOOD LUCK!!

TP
YAH!
TP
YO!
TP
HOI!
TAH--!!
PYOONG
GASP
HE'S AMAZING...
HE'S ALREADY OUT OF SIGHT...

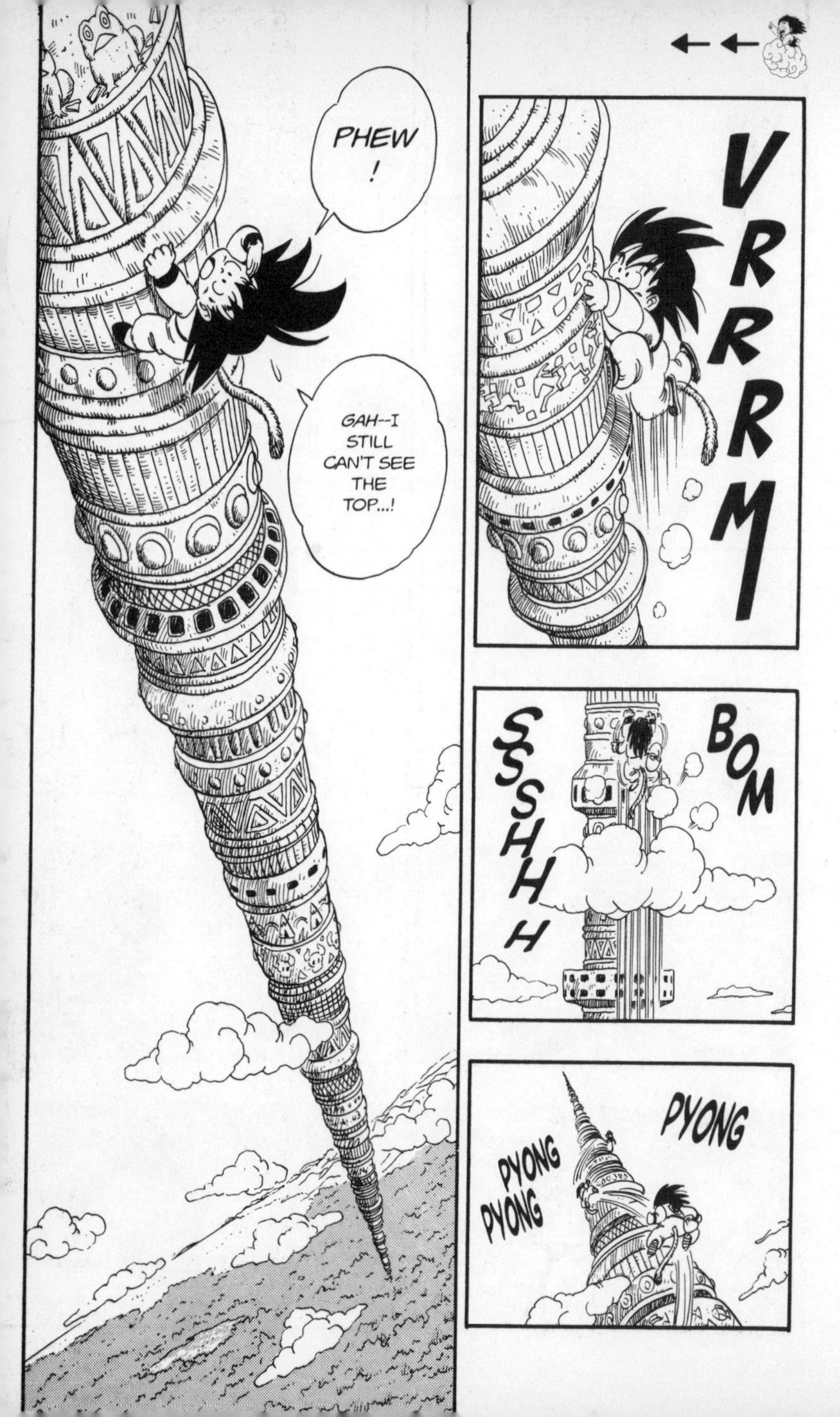

VRRRM
SSSHHH
BOM
PYONG
PYONG
PYONG
PYONG
PHEW!
GAH--I STILL CAN'T SEE THE TOP...!

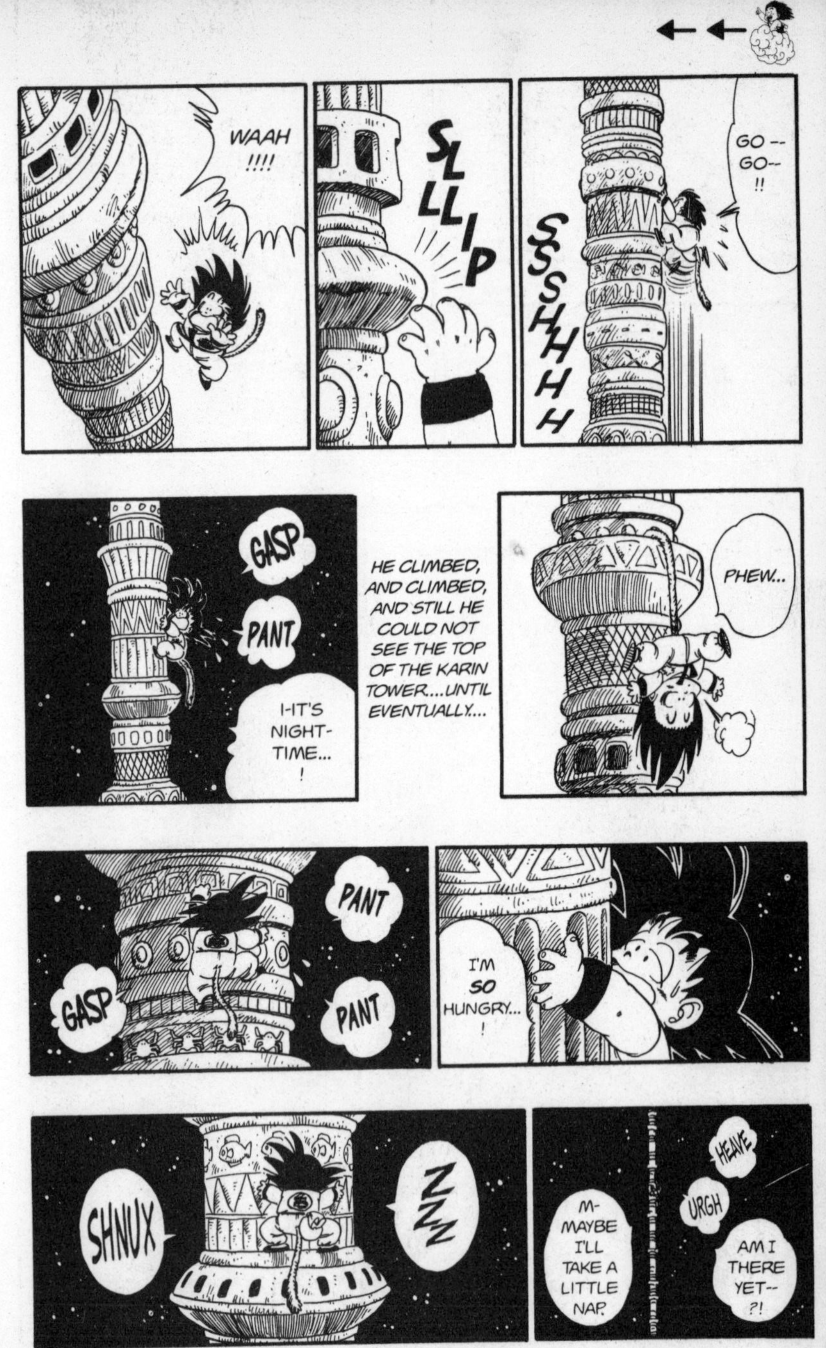
GO -- GO-- !!
SSSHHHHH
SLLIP
WAAH !!!!
PHEW...
HE CLIMBED, AND CLIMBED, AND STILL HE COULD NOT SEE THE TOP OF THE KARIN TOWER....UNTIL EVENTUALLY....
GASP
PANT
I-IT'S NIGHT-TIME... !
I'M SO HUNGRY... !
PANT
PANT
GASP
HEAVE
URGH
AM I THERE YET-- ?!
M-MAYBE I'LL TAKE A LITTLE NAP.
ZZZ
SHNUX

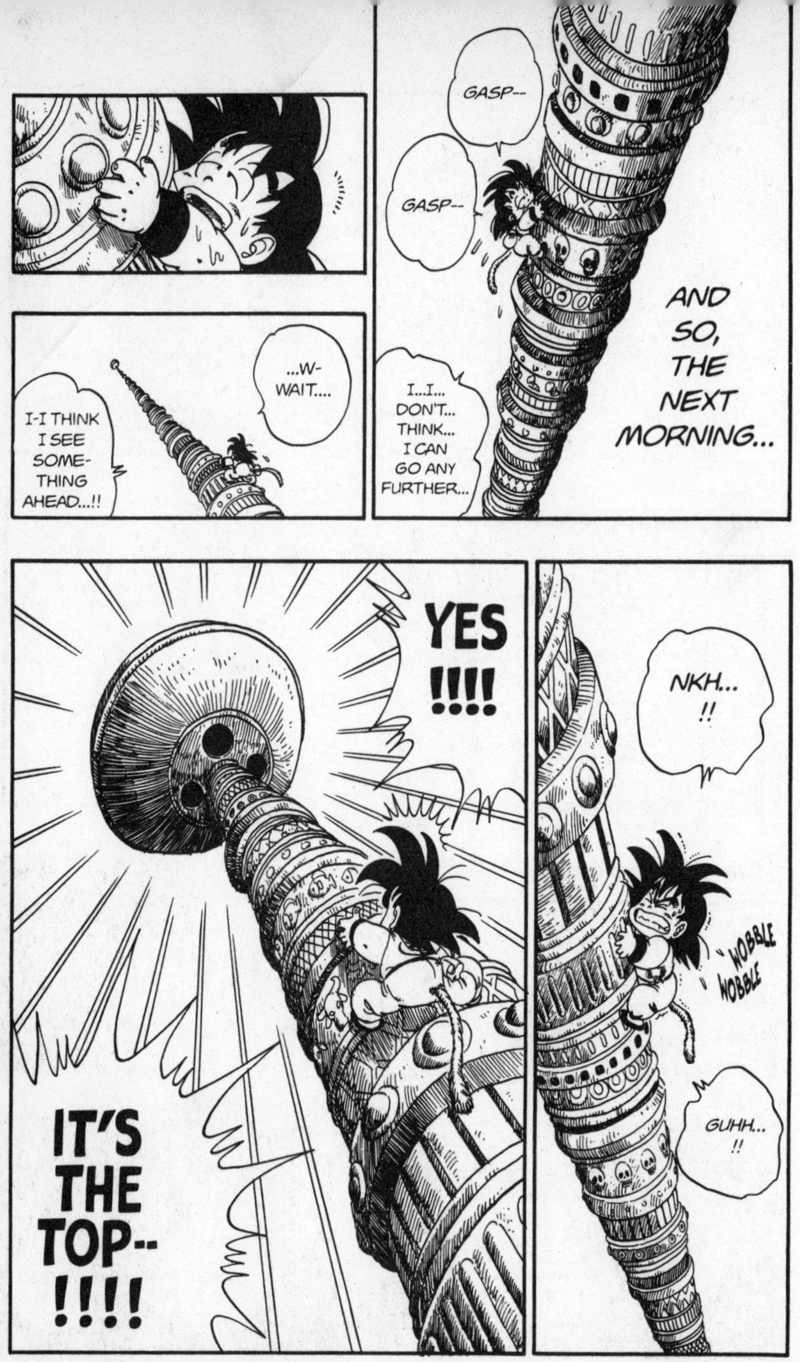

NEXT: Karin-Sen'nin

Tale 88 • Sage of the Karin Tower

HUFF HUFF
PANT PANT
IS THIS IT... ?
...SO WHERE'S THIS MAGIC WATER THAT'S SUPPOSED TO MAKE YOU STRONGER...?
OH, THAT'S RIGHT... HE SAID THERE WAS A HERMIT LIVING HERE....
IT'S UP HERE-- COME ON UP!
HUH ?

HEY-- MR. HERMIT MASTER! GIMME SOME WATER, PLEASE!
CONGRAT-ULATIONS ON REACHING THE TOP!
AND SO QUICKLY, TOO.... ESPECIALLY FOR A LITTLE SQUIRT LIKE YOU....

HUH ?
WHO ARE YOU CALLING A SQUIRT, SHORTY?!
OH, BE QUIET.
WHERE'S THE HERMIT MASTER ?
YOU'RE LOOKING AT HIM.
WHAT?! *YOU'RE* THE HERMIT MASTER?!
NOT WHAT YOU EX-PECTED ?
IT'S TRUE, PERHAPS I SHOULD CALL MYSELF A HERMIT MEOWSTER.... HO HO HO....
WELL, I GUESS IT DOESN'T MATTER...
ALL I WANT TO KNOW ABOUT IS THIS WATER THAT'S SUPPOSED TO MULTIPLY YOUR STRENGTH! THAT'S WHAT I CAME FOR!
AHHH.... YOU MUST MEAN THE HOLY WATER....
IT'S HERE, INDEED...

...IN THAT FLASK, SITTING RIGHT ON TOP OF THAT PODIUM....
BUT WAIT... DO YOU SEEK FURTHER STRENGTH? YOU MUST BE AWFULLY STRONG AS IT IS.
WELL, YOU SEE, MY GRAM-PA...
NEVER MIND. YOU DON'T HAVE TO EXPLAIN.
SPEECH ISN'T YOUR STRONG SUIT, I SUSPECT.
I DON'T HAVE TO...? BUT YOU'RE THE ONE WHO ASKED!
REALLY! YOU DON'T HAVE TO SAY A WORD!

...
I SEE--
IN ORDER TO GATHER THE DRAGON BALLS AND REVIVE UPA'S FATHER...
YOU MUST FIRST DEFEAT THIS KILLER NAMED TAOPAIPAI...

H-HEY!! HOW'D YOU FIGURE THAT OUT?!
IF I COULDN'T READ YOUR MIND, I WOULDN'T BE MUCH OF A HERMIT MASTER.
WELL, ALL RIGHT.
YOU DO SEEM TO HAVE PURE MOTIVES, AT LEAST!
WOW...
MIND READING, HUH....?
SO IT'S OKAY IF I TAKE SOME OF THIS SUPER WATER?
I'LL BE HAPPY TO GIVE YOU SOME... BUT DO YOU THINK YOU'LL BE ABLE TO DRINK IT?
HUH? DOES IT TASTE THAT BAD?!
NOT REALLY, NO. IT'S JUST THAT I'M GOING TO PREVENT YOU FROM DRINKING.
PREVENT?
HYAH!

TOP
HWRRR
WAAH !!
DOM
HEY-- WHAT WAS THAT ALL ABOUT ?!!
IF YOU WANT THE HOLY WATER, TRY TO TAKE THE FLASK AND DRINK IT!
SSHHH
HYUUUNN
GEEZ YOU'RE ANNOYING...
OKAY THEN.... !!!

PAM!
I'M NO CHEAPSKATE-- BUT IN ORDER TO DRINK THE HOLY WATER, FIRST YOU MUST PROVE YOU ARE WORTHY OF IT-- IN COMBAT!!
YOU CHEAP-SKATE!! I THOUGHT YOU SAID I COULD DRINK IT!!
TUP
HUH ?
LOOK-- !!!
GONG
VSSH

PWIII
LOOK.
OWW-- !!
AIEE AIEE
DO YOU REALLY THINK THAT A HERMIT MASTER WHO CAN READ MINDS WOULD FALL FOR THAT STUPID TRICK?
SLOSH SLOSH
HERE, HERE.
NO, NO, OVER HERE.
NOW YOU'VE GOT ME MAD!!
I'M JUST GONNA TAKE THAT WATER !!
TYAH-- !!
FWAAA
WHOOPS!

NYAH NYAH
WHOOPS!
WHOOPS!
HA!
CATCH ME IF YOU CAN--
PANT PANT
H- HE'S FAST...!!
AT THE RATE YOU'RE GOING, YOU MAY HAVE THIS FLASK BY YOUR NEXT LIFE.
YOU'RE NOT READING YOUR OPPONENT'S MOVES AT ALL! YOU'RE ONLY REACTING!
WH- WHAT THE--
IF I WEREN'T STARVING, I COULD BEAT YOU JUST LIKE THAT!
OH?
WELL THEN, I'LL LET YOU EAT.

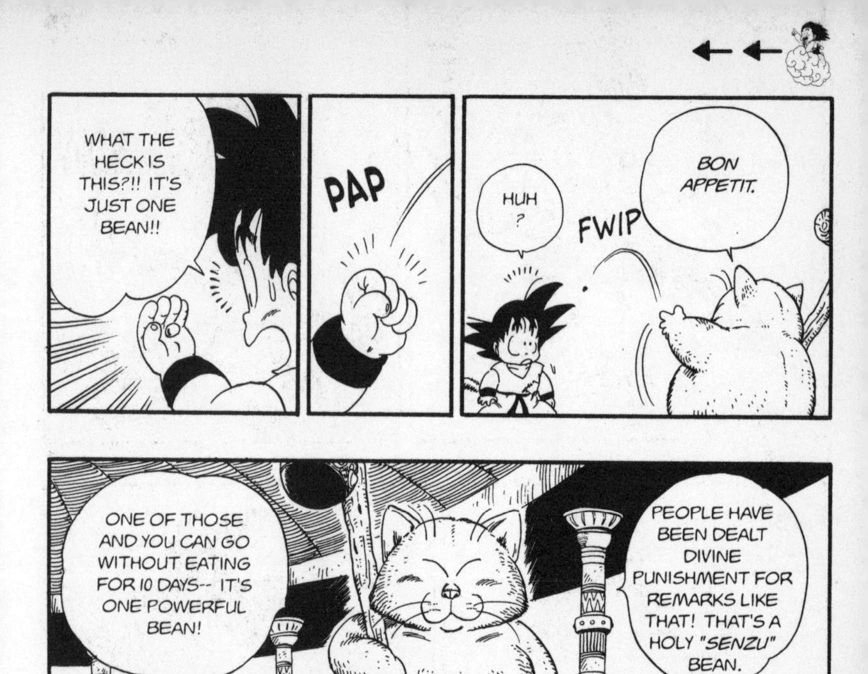
BON APPETIT.
HUH?
FWIP
PAP
WHAT THE HECK IS THIS?!! IT'S JUST ONE BEAN!!
PEOPLE HAVE BEEN DEALT DIVINE PUNISHMENT FOR REMARKS LIKE THAT! THAT'S A HOLY "SENZU" BEAN.
ONE OF THOSE AND YOU CAN GO WITHOUT EATING FOR 10 DAYS-- IT'S ONE POWERFUL BEAN!

THIS THING...?
MNCH MNCH
IT TAKES A LOT MORE THAN THIS TO FILL ME UP...
GULP
SIGH

WH-WHAT THE--?!!
I-IT'S TRUE!! I CAN'T BELIEVE IT...!!
HEH HEH HEH! YOUR LOSS! NOW THAT MY STOMACH'S FULL, THE FLASK IS MINE!
TSK TSK. POOR ME.

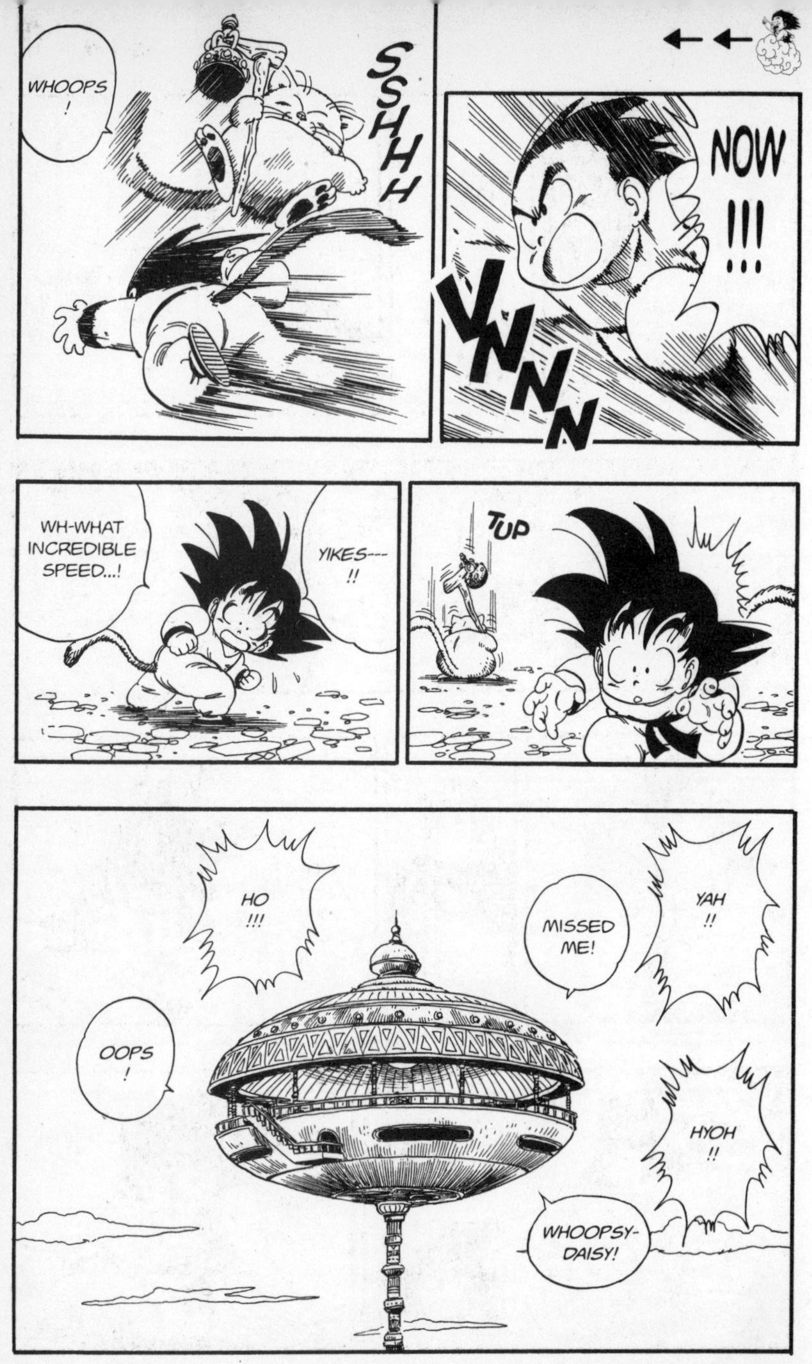
NOW !!!
VNNN
SSHHH
WHOOPS !
YIKES--- !!
WH-WHAT INCREDIBLE SPEED...!
TUP
YAH !!
MISSED ME!
HO !!!
HYOH !!
WHOOPSY-DAISY!
OOPS !

PANT PANT
GASP GASP
WHAT-- TIRED ALREADY ?
H-HEY...AM I THE...FIRST ONE TO CLIMB UP HERE...?
OH NO, YOU'RE NOT THE FIRST.
ABOUT 300 YEARS AGO, THERE WAS ONE OTHER WHO WAS ABLE TO SCALE THE TOWER.
H-HOW OLD *ARE* YOU?
LET'S JUST SAY...800 SOME-THING.
MAN.... YOU ARE *OLD*!!
YOU SHOULD RESPECT ME!
THE ONE OTHER FELLOW WHO WAS ABLE TO SCALE THE TOWER....
...WAS YOUR MENTOR.
HUH ?!
WHAT DO YOU MEAN ?!
I CAN TELL BY OBSERVING YOUR MOVES.
YOUR MASTER IS THE MUTEN-RŌSHI, ISN'T HE?

NEXT: The Secret of the Magic Water

OKAY, SO.... TO BRING UPA'S DAD BACK TO LIFE, GOKU HAS TO GET ALL THE DRAGON BALLS, WHICH MEANS HE HAS TO DEFEAT TAOPAIPAI, WHICH MEANS HE HAS TO INCREASE HIS STRENGTH, WHICH MEANS HE HAS TO DRINK THE HOLY WATER...

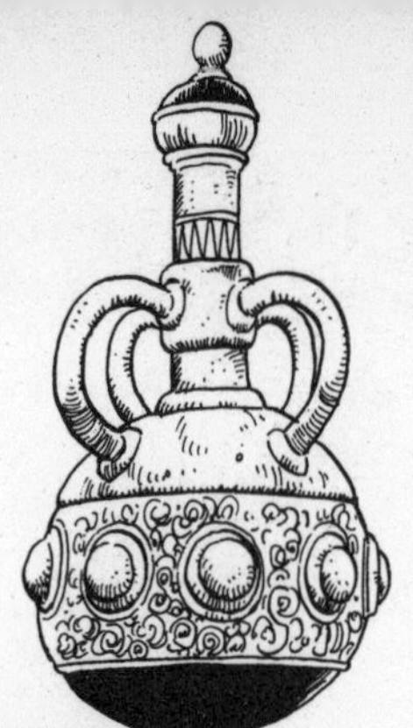

WHICH MEANS HE HAS TO STEAL THE FLASK FROM MASTER KARIN WHO'S ONLY BEEN BEATEN ONCE BEFORE AND THAT WAS BY THE INVINCIBLE OLD MASTER, AND IT TOOK HIM....

Tale 89 • A Drink of Water

WELL, IF YOU CAN'T WAIT, YOU SHOULD JUST HURRY UP AND STEAL THIS HOLY WATER.
THAT'S ALL IT WOULD TAKE, RIGHT?

ALL RIGHT--!! I'LL **DO** IT!!
TYAH--!!
KWRRRRR

VNNN
VNNN
VNNN
VNNN

HO! A SPLIT-IMAGE ILLUSION MOVE, HM?

HO HO HO...

VWAAA
YOU'RE RIGHT THERE !!!
SSHHH
HUH ?!
TOO BAD-- I WAS OVER HERE--!!

GO
NG
SHWAAA
EEP ?!
MEOW-HAHA!
OWW--!!
I TURNED YOUR SPLIT-IMAGE BACK AGAINST YOU!
DID YOU THINK I WOULDN'T SEE THROUGH THAT?
THIS COULD BE QUITE INTERESTING...
THIS LAD IS PRETTY GOOD... I'VE NEVER SEEN SO MANY SPLIT IMAGES IN THAT MOVE BEFORE...
YOU PUT TOO MUCH EXTRA MOVEMENT IN YOUR MOVES, WHICH COSTS YOU BREATH.
WE'RE AT QUITE A HIGH ALTITUDE, YOU KNOW. THE AIR IS THIN.
HUF...HUF... HOW COME I'M OUT OF BREATH ALREADY...?

HUH? WHAT ARE YOU TALKING ABOUT ?
I'LL HAVE TO TEACH YOU SOME THINGS, I SEE.
CLIMBING THIS VERY TALL TOWER HAS BEEN GOOD FOR YOUR LUNG CONDITIONING, I SUSPECT....
YOU THINK SO...?
OH, YES, YES. BUT YOU'LL NEED A LITTLE MORE CONDITIONING THAN THAT....
HUH ?
HEY!! THE POUCH WITH MY DRAGON BALL...!! WHEN DID YOU TAKE THAT?!
AND WHAT ARE YOU GONNA DO?! GIVE IT BACK!!

HERE.
POI!!!
WACK!!
WHAT DO YOU THINK YOU'RE-- ?!!!
HYOOON
YOU'RE CRAZY-- !!!!
FSH
SHEESH !!
IF THE RED RIBBON ARMY GOT AHOLD OF THAT BALL, IT'D BE AWFUL!!!
TMM
THERE IT IS!!
PHEW-- !!

THAT CONCEITED CAT!!
I'M GONNA MAKE IT YOWL!!!
VSSSN!
WHAT'S THE IDEA, MAKING ME GO THROUGH ALL THAT ?!!
PANT PANT !!
DON'T YOU APPRECIATE THE EXTRA TRAINING ?
HO HO HO...
IT TOOK YOU ALMOST A WHOLE DAY TO CLIMB THE TOWER THE FIRST TIME....
BUT JUST NOW YOU MADE THE ROUND TRIP IN ABOUT THREE HOURS.... THAT'S SOME PROGRESS!
...
W-WELL.... I GUESS....

NOW... BACK TO BUSI-NESS--
STEAL THE FLASK AND DRINK THE HOLY WATER.
...
OH YEAH...
TAH!
YAH!
HO- YOU'RE GETTING BETTER AT KEEPING UP WITH ME NOW--
BUT YOU'RE STILL FAR FROM STEALING IT....
PANT PANT
GASP
WHY DON'T WE CALL IT A DAY? I'M SLEEPY.
ZZZ
ZZZ

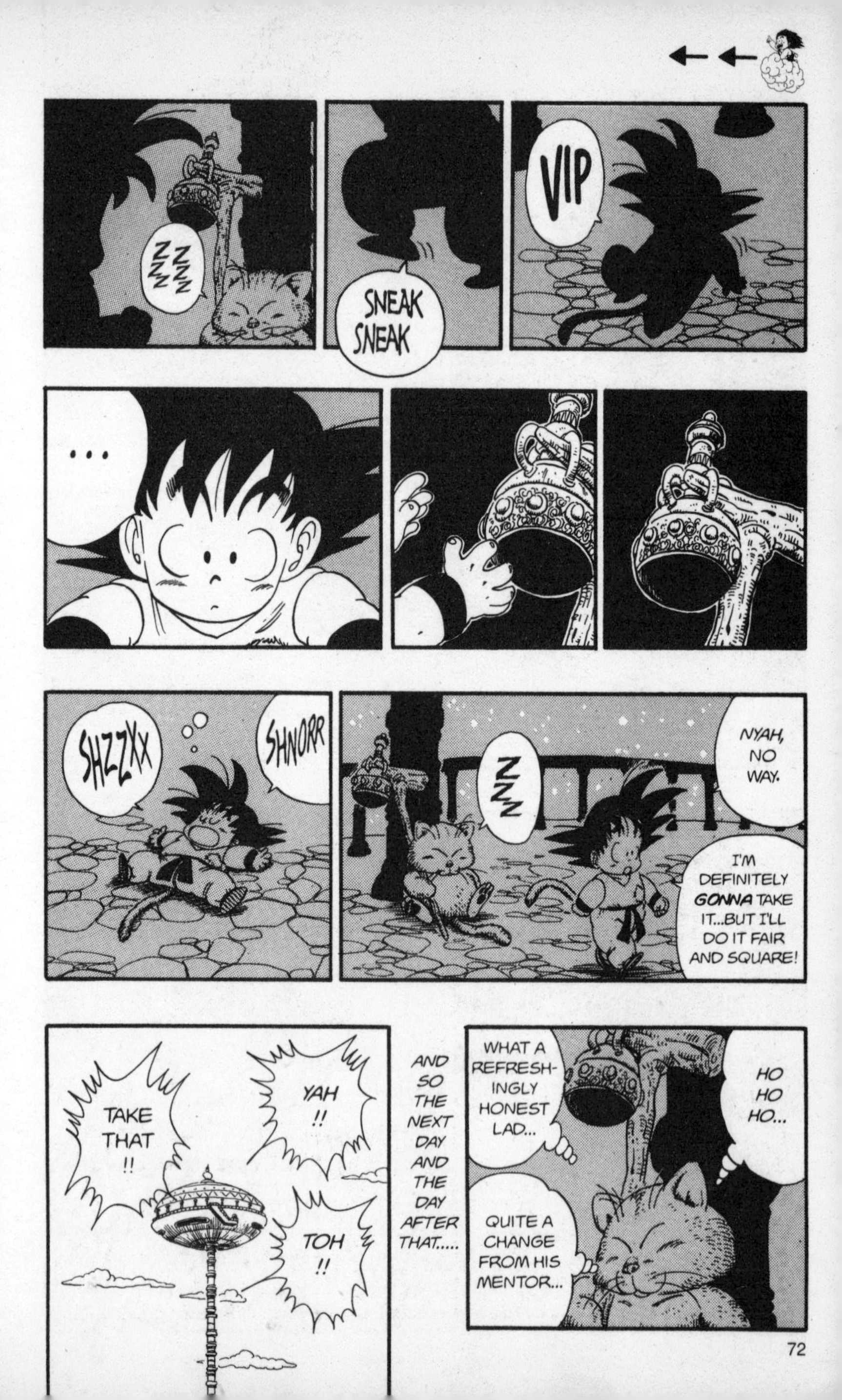
VIP
SNEAK SNEAK
ZZZ ZZZ
...
NYAH, NO WAY.
ZZZ
I'M DEFINITELY **GONNA** TAKE IT...BUT I'LL DO IT FAIR AND SQUARE!
SHNORR
SHZZXX
HO HO HO...
WHAT A REFRESH-INGLY HONEST LAD...
QUITE A CHANGE FROM HIS MENTOR...
AND SO THE NEXT DAY AND THE DAY AFTER THAT.....
YAH !!
TAKE THAT !!
TOH !!

ALL RIGHT! TODAY IS THE DAY I WILL TAKE THAT FLASK!
HAH !!
BASSSH
PAP
VNNN
HAII !!!
FWAA
TOH !!!

GYA-HAHA-HAHA-HA!!!
TICKLE TICKLE
OH !!
BONG
SH-SHOOT !!!

IT'S NOT WORTH IT !!!
YOU'LL FALL !!!!
GRAB
WAAH-- ...!
L- LAD !!!
OH !!
JUST KIDDING !
YAY-- !!!
I GOT THE FLASK-- !!
WH-WHAT AN ASTON-ISHING CHILD....
TO HAVE DONE IT IN JUST THREE DAYS... !

I CAN DRINK IT, RIGHT ?!
OF COURSE-- GO AHEAD, DRINK IT
HEH HEH HEH--
POP
GLUP
GLUP
GLUP
...?
...?
HEY... I DON'T REALLY FEEL ANY DIFFERENT....
OF COURSE NOT.
THE "HOLY WATER" IS JUST ORDINARY RAIN WATER.
HUH?
WHAT-- ?!
Y-YOU MEAN YOU TRICKED ME?!! WHAT A MEAN, LOW----

NEXT: Son Goku's Revenge

Tale 90 • Son Goku Strikes Back!
GLANCE GLANCE
TROT TROT TROT

YES, YES, JUST AS I INSTRUCTED....
EXCEL-LENT.
I WENT WITHOUT SLEEP TO FINISH IT!
I SUPPOSE I SHOULD HEAD OFF TO FIND THAT LAST DRAGON BALL OR WHATEVER IT IS...
NOW THEN...
IT'S BEEN THREE DAYS ALREADY... I WONDER IF GOKU WAS ABLE TO GET TO THE TOP...

UM... M-MY FEE...?
TWIK
YOU...
...EXPECT TO TAKE MONEY FROM TAOPAIPAI, THE WORLD'S GREATEST ASSASSIN?!
B-BUT... I HAVE TO MAKE A LIVING TOO...
ALL RIGHT, THEN, LET'S DO THIS. I'M A KILLER. SO INSTEAD OF MONEY, I'LL KILL SOMEONE FOR YOU!
YOU DON'T KNOW HOW LUCKY YOU ARE! MY HIT FEE IS MORE THAN A LOWLY CITIZEN LIKE YOU COULD AFFORD IF YOU WORKED EVERY DAY FOR THE REST OF YOUR LIFE! NOW...WHO'LL IT BE?
N-NO!!
THERE'S NOBODY I WANT TO KILL!!
WELL THEN... WOULD YOU LIKE TO DIE?
JABB

KEEP THE CHANGE.
DNNN
KRAM
!!
TUP
GASP !!

YOU AGAIN!! I MUST AVENGE FATHER!!
HYAH!!!
VNNN
HAND IT OVER.
THERE SHOULD BE ONE OF THOSE BALLS ROLLING AROUND HERE SOME-WHERE.
YAAH!!!
PAMM
ZIP

GRAB
PERHAPS YOU DIDN'T HEAR ME!
WHERE IS THE BALL !?
NNH... NNGH... !!
KI
I-I'LL... NEVER... TELL YOU...!!
IN THAT CASE, I'LL JUST KILL YOU RIGHT HERE.
AFTER ALL, I CAN ALWAYS USE THAT RADAR GADGET TO LOCATE THE BALL, EH?
...
WHAT A STUBBORN BRAT. ALL RIGHT THEN, HAVE IT YOUR WAY.
VNNN
WAAH !!!
KI
!!!

KINTO'-UN!!!
FWA
VYOOON
OOONNNN

OH !!!
MADE IT--!!!
WHAT... !!!
...IN THE WORLD... ?!!!

G-GOKU!!
THAT'S WHY I TOLD YOU TO HIDE!
THIS MUST BE A JOKE...
HE COULDN'T HAVE...
YOU MADE IT TO THE TOP?! YOU GOT TO DRINK THE HOLY WATER?!!
YUP!! I'M BETTER'N EVER NOW!!
YAAAAAY!!!
YOU JUST STAY UP HERE ON MY CLOUD, OKAY?
YES, SIR!!
SO... YOU'RE STILL ALIVE, EH...?!
TUP
YOU WANT THE DRAGON BALL?
WELL, YOU AREN'T GETTIN' IT!

HOW'D YOU DO IT, BOY ?!
NO ONE SURVIVES TAOPAIPAI'S DODON-PA!
I WAS SAVED BY THE DRAGON BALL IN MY SHIRT POCKET!
I SEE... *HEH HEH HEH*... WHAT A LUCKY FELLOW YOU ARE...
IF YOU'D BEEN HIT BY THAT BLAST YOU'D BE DEAD AS THAT DRAGON BALL!
BUT THIS... IS WHERE YOUR LUCK RUNS OUT.
NOTHING WILL SAVE YOU NOW. YOU SHOULD HAVE STAYED IN HIDING, FOOL!
NOW HAND OVER THE BALL....
...OR WOULD YOU RATHER DIE FOR *REAL* THIS TIME ?!
I *WON'T* HAND IT OVER !
AND I WON'T LET YOU KNOCK ME AROUND AGAIN EITHER!

HAHAHA... YOU LITTLE NINCOM-POOP !
YOU'LL BE DEAD IN THREE SECONDS !!
DOM
HAIYAH !!!!
HWAA
VVVV

DONK
UGH !!!
TOMM
BOMM
FYOOOOON
BWAK
NKH !!!
KILL YOU!!

GAH !!!
GLAM
...WOW...
...GOKU... !
TMP
TOP
I THINK YOUR THREE SECONDS IS UP BY NOW!!
WH- WHAT... ?!
YOU WEREN'T DOING ANY-THING LIKE THIS THREE DAYS AGO!
WHAT'S HAPPENING HERE.... ?!
THAT'S CUZ I WASN'T HIDING--
I WAS TRAINING AT THE TOP OF THAT POLE !!
TRAIN-ING... AT THE TOP ... ?!
NO THREE DAYS OF TRAINING COULD DO THIS!!

NEXT: Goku vs. Taopaipai, Take Two!

Tale 91 • Battle in the Sanctuary!!
HEH HEH HEH... NOW SEE WHAT HAPPENS TO THOSE WHO UNDER-ESTIMATE TAOPAIPAI !!
QUIT YAKKING AND MAKE YOUR MOVE!!
OOOOO, ARE YOU ANNOYING... !!
NOW I'M GOING TO GET SERIOUS !!
FINALLY !!
GOOD LUCK, GOKU-- !!
TSOH !!!!

KRAK
KRAK
BOOF
YAH!!
BWAK
TUP
HEH HEH--
...UGH...!

Y...
YOU--... !!
HAI !!!!! !!!!
VMM
GNNN
THOOM

UGH!!
WHOK
THOP
BMMM
DWOK

TMMM
KRAKKA
TNNNN
THWOG

TUP
POP
RRRRIP
INGRATE! I HOLD BACK BECAUSE YOU'RE A CHILD AND WHAT DO YOU DO?! TAKE ADVANTAGE OF ME!!
YOU SAID YOU WERE GONNA BE SERIOUS!

ALL RIGHT... THIS TIME I'M SERIOUSLY SERIOUS !!!
TAOPAIPAI'S ULTIMATE MOVE...THE DODON BLAST!!!!!
DODON-PA!!!
G-GOKU !!!
LOOK OUT !!!
!!

ZZIP
SHWA
HWOOOO
C'MON!!! GIMME YOUR BEST!!!

BAM
ZUD-D-D-D-!!
QUIVER
QUIVER...
PUFF
PUFF
OWWW
!!

TWITCH TWITCH
N... NO.....
YOU DON'T MEAN...
M-MY DODONPA...
HEY! MY KAMEHAMEHA DIDN'T WORK AGAINST YOU...
...AND YOUR DOO-DOO THINGIE DOESN'T WORK AGAINST ME!
HE DID IT!!
YOU... !!
GRAB
PING

WAAA !!
TYAA !!!
SSHHHH
SWIP
BOM
A CAPSULE !
HYAA !!!
FYOOOOO
WHOA, WHOA !!
HO !!!
YIPE !!!
SPLASH

WAHAHA! EVEN YOU ARE NO MATCH FOR MY BLADE!!
EEP---
HAA !!
TAA !!!
AUGH !!
HOP
TEP
OWW !!
DASH
SNATCH
G- GOKU !!!!
FLINNNG

!!
MY NYOI-BÔ !!!
THANKS !!
BONG
FWASH
SSSS
DYAH-- !!!

NEXT: Monkey vs. Assassin!

Tale 92 • Taopaipai at the Brink

I PROMISE TO AVENGE YOUR DAD, UPA !!
I KNOW YOU WILL, GOKU!!
Y-YOU MAKE LIGHT OF ME....
YOU WILL BE SORRY !!!
TSUAH!!!!
FYOO

BWOK
GOG
TOON
BUDDA
BUDDA
BUDDA
VWOO

WH-
WHAT'S
HAP-
PENING,
GOKU--
?!!
WHY
ARE YOU
JUST
LETTING
HIM HIT
YOU
?!
SEI-
YAH
!!!
DWOOG
HYAAH
!!!
LEAP

CHA-!!!!!!
BWAKK
ZUH-BOOM
SNEER
AND NOW-- THE FINAL STRIKE !!!!
HWOOO!

WHRL
!!
AARGH!!!
DOOF!!
HEH...

HAHAHA !!!
DEAD AT LAST, EH ?!!
BY THE TIME YOU REALIZED WHAT YOU WERE UP AGAINST, IT WAS ALREADY TOO LATE !!!
MWIP
HUH ?
MAN! YOU ARE GOOD !
THAT REALLY HURT !
!!
GOKU !!
Y-
YOU'RE A MONSTER !!!

BUT NOW I'VE SEEN ALL YOUR MOVES!!
AND I KNOW HOW TO FIGHT BACK!!!
HYAH!!!!
YOU--
IMPU-DENT--
LITTLE--
!!!!
DOOOM
ZMMMM

KWAM
KRAAK
DOMMM
TAP
GAG
NNNNH...
!!

HIS SPEED... IS IMPOSSIBLE !!
TH-THERE HAS TO BE SOME EXPLANATION.... !!!
HERE I COME AGAIN !!
I-I'M FINISHED... UNLESS... !!
WAIT!!! I'M SORRY !!!
FOR-GIVE ME !!!
I SWEAR I'LL NEVER COMMIT EVIL DEEDS AGAIN!!
HUH ?!
...

PLEASE!! HAVE MERCY !!
B-BUT GEEZ... AFTER EVERYTHING YOU'VE DONE... ?
WHAT DO YOU WANT TO DO... ?
...
WA-HAHAHA-HAHA!!!
YOU FELL FOR IT!!!!
VOOON
WHAT-- ?!
IT'S A BOMB-- !!!!

FARE-
WELL---
FOOLS
!!!
DIVE
KLONK

KRAK
NO...
EH--
?!

BAKOOOOM!!
UGH
!!!

NEXT: Goku's Charge!

Tale 93 • Goku's Charge

AFTER GAINING TREMENDOUS POWER ON THE KARIN TOWER, GOKU FINALLY TOOK DOWN TAOPAIPAI! NOW HE PLANS TO CONTINUE HIS QUEST FOR DRAGON BALLS SO THAT HE CAN USE THEM TO RESURRECT UPA'S MURDERED FATHER... BUT THERE ARE THREE BALLS LEFT AND HIS NEXT TARGET IS...

THIS IS PERFECT!!
I CAN BEAT THEM ALL UP WHILE I'M AT IT!!!
B-B-BUT THAT'S TOO MUCH EVEN FOR YOU, GOKU! TO TAKE ON THE RED RIBBON ARMY ALONE...
WELL, I GOTTA GO THERE TO GET THE BALLS ANYWAY, RIGHT?
JUST DON'T GET INTO ANYTHING MORE DANGEROUS THAN YOU HAVE TO, OKAY?
OH, FOOEY, DON'T WORRY ABOUT ME!
KINTO-UN~!
RED RIBBON ARMY HQ
RR

COMMANDER RED, COLONEL VIOLET HAS RETURNED WITH THE DRAGON BALL.
MMM!
MISSION ACCOMPLISHED!
SORRY IT TOOK SO LONG TO FIND, SIR!
EX--CELLENT! NOW, WHEN TAOPAIPAI RETURNS, WE'LL HAVE SIX OF THE SEVEN!
THE PRECISION OF THE ENEMY'S RADAR IS QUITE IMPRESSIVE.
WE WERE ABLE TO LOCATE THE TARGET ALMOST INSTANTANEOUSLY.
VERY WELL--GIVE THAT RADAR TO GENERAL COPPER AND ORDER HIM TO FIND THE LAST DRAGON BALL IMMEDIATELY!
EH?
COMMANDER... THOSE FOUR BALLS... THEY'RE MOVING!
MOVING?
IT'S TAOPAIPAI....

WHAT'S THAT ?
HUH ?
HYUUUUUN

WHAT A WEIRDO...
HYUU-U UN

KAME HOUSE

THERE HE IS! IT'S GOKU !!
WHAT ?!!
PII
PIPIII

HE'S ALIVE!
HO--! INDEED, INDEED!
BEER
IS HE PLANNING TO COME BACK HERE, I WONDER ?
KWIII
LET ME CHECK IT OUT.
ZZZHHH
PING
NOPE...
LOOKS LIKE HE'S HEADING TOWARDS WHERE THESE TWO DRAGON BALLS ARE!
YOU'D THINK HE COULD AT LEAST STOP AND SAY HI !
THAT LOCA-TION...
YOU REALLY ARE AMAZING, THOUGH... FINDING RANDOM MATERIALS, PULLING THEM TOGETHER INTO SOMETHING THIS BRILLIANT.... TOO BAD YOU'RE BUILT LIKE A BOY!
ALWAYS ONE COMMENT TOO MANY !!!

AM I WRONG OR....
...IS HE HEADING FOR RED RIBBON ARMY HEAD-QUARTERS ?
WHAT ?!
NO WAY... NOT EVEN GOKU....
I'LL CHECK IT OUT !!
CHECK IT OUT... HOW ?
BP BP BP
I'LL SEND THE RECON MECH TO WHERE THE TWO BALLS ARE!
HEY, WHAT'S UP WITH YOU, DUDE? WHY ARE YOU FOLLOWING ME?
KCH CHK CHK CHK CHK CHK
BABYOOON

CHEEZ...
HE'S EVEN FASTER THAN KINTO'UN...!
WE SHOULD BE APPROACHING THE RIGHT AREA ABOUT NOW.
LET ME SWITCH TO VISUALS.

D-DON'T TELL ME HE'S P-PLANNING TO INVADE THAT...?!
IT'S THEIR CENTRAL COMMAND...
...ULP... YOU WERE RIGHT...
RR
DOOOM
BSHOOOO
WE HAVE JUST ENGAGED A UFO.
THIS IS UNIT 84, THIS IS UNIT 84--
84
AWP!! WE'VE BEEN HIT !!
ZZZHHH
DON'T WORRY, DON'T WORRY. IT WAS JUST A MINIATURE RECON UNIT OR SOME SUCH.
NO!! IT'S TAOPAIPAI!! HE'S COMING OUR WAY !!

THE FOUR DRAGON BALLS HAVE ARRIVED !
AT LAST, TAOPAIPAI HAS ARRIVED WITH HIS TROPHIES!
AH HA!! THAT'S THE PLACE!!!
O--- KAY-- !!
LET'S HAVE SOME FUN !!!!

GYUUUN
ALL RIGHT, HERE'S TAOPAIPAI....
N-NO !!!!
IT'S NOT TAOPAI-PAI-- !!!!
WHAT ARE WE GONNA DO?!
NOT EVEN GOKU'S STRONG ENOUGH TO HANDLE THE WHOLE RED RIBBON ARMY!! HE'LL BE SLAUGHTERED !!
NO, NO.... JUST STUPID...
I SUPPOSE OUR ONLY CHOICE IS TO GO HELP HIM.
HE MUST BE INSANE... !
AND HOW, MAY I ASK, WILL YOU GET THERE?
OH, THAT'S RIGHT !
WE DON'T HAVE ANY TRANSPORTATION LEFT HERE, DO WE...?

SHEESH !!
IF I COULD ONLY CONTACT YAMCHA... !!
WHY DON'T YOU TELEPHONE HIM?
AND DO YOU SEE A PHONE HERE ?!!!
BUT MA'AM, IF YOU COULD BUILD THAT...
THEN SURELY SOMETHING AS SIMPLE AS A TELEPHONE SHOULDN'T BE.....?
OH YEAH!! THAT'S RIGHT !!!
YOU'RE SO SMART !!!
CLANG KACLANG BANG
IT'S A THIN LINE BETWEEN IDIOCY AND GENIUS....
YES !!!
KCHAK CHAK-CHAK-CHAK
HUL-LOA ?!
FATHER!! IT'S ME, BULMA!! IS YAMCHA HOME ?!
BULMA! LONG TIME NO SPEAK! OH, THIS IS PERFECT, I JUST CAME UP WITH A HILARIOUS JOKE! LISTEN TO THIS....
WILL YOU JUST PUT YAMCHA ON ?!!!

WH-WHAT?! GOKU'S TAKING ON THE WHAT... ?!
BUT IT'S SUCH A GOOD JOKE...
WHERE HAVE YOU BEEN? I THOUGHT YOU WENT TO SEARCH FOR DRAGON BALLS WITH GOKU.
I THINK I'LL JUST GO OVER HERE...
SNEAK SNEAK
THIS CAN'T BE GOOD IF HE'S SO EXCITED...
UH-HUH... YEAH....GOT IT!! I'LL LEAVE RIGHT AWAY!!
THE RED RIBBON ARMY... ?!!!
TH-...
PU'AR! OOLONG! WE'RE GOING TO GO HELP GOKU!! WE'RE RIDING INTO THE RED RIBBON ARMY!!!
THIS'LL BE QUITE A CHANGE FROM THIS CITY OF COWARDS....
WHAT AN INCREDIBLE OPPONENT...
PWIK

KABOO--M
UNIT 84, RESPOND!!...
HE'S... HE'S BEEN TAKEN OUT...!! WHAT'S GOING ON?!!
INITIATE LASER MONITOR!!
YES, SIR!!
PAP
OH!!!!
C-COMMANDER!!! THE POSSESSOR OF THE BALLS IS NOT TAOPAIPAI!!! IT'S THAT KID... SON GOKU!!!
WH-WHAT...?!!!

Tale 94 • Attack from the Sky!

ALL---
RIGHT
!!!!
CHAA-
AAAAA-
ARGE--
!!
GYOOO!
WHAT IS THAT BRAT DOING HERE ?!!!!
IT CAN'T MEAN... BUT IT HAS TO MEAN.... HE DEFEATED THE TERRIBLE TAOPAIPAI....
RR

DON'T LET HIM PENETRATE!! NOT A SINGLE STEP!!
HE'S ALREADY IN!! HE'S ON SECTOR 12'S TERRACE!!
...GRRR.... !
B-KRAK
RAT-TAT-TAT-TAT!!
BLAM

DOP DOP
TWA
PIP
THAT WAY, I'LL BET!

THERE HE IS OVER THERE !!
DMDMDM
HYUUUN HYUUUN
PYONG
DM DM
PAPAPA

BABABABABA
OH !!!
DOMPF
GAH !!
KONG
HAI-YAA !!
LEAP
HYUUN
BABABA

WHOOPS !!
KA
ME
HA
ME...
BOOOM
FEH !!!
BA-BA-BA
HAA !!!
DOM
WHA-- ?!

BOMF
WAAH !!!
DOOOM
VVVV
N-NO !!
PAPAPA
OVER HERE!! HE'S ON THE GROUND--!!

HE'S HEADING STRAIGHT FOR TOWER 8!!
SO HE DOES WANT THE DRAGON BALLS, JUST AS I SUSPECTED...
COMMANDER!! PLEASE EVACUATE TO THE UNDER-GROUND BUNKER, JUST IN CASE!!
YOU'VE GOT TO BE KIDDING!! ME?!! HIDE FROM ONE STUPID LITTLE BRAT?!!!
A BRAT...WHO WAS ABLE TO DEFEAT TAOPAIPAI....
THE RED RIBBON ARMY IS AN IN-VINCIBLE FORCE !!!
ZUDD
RAT-TAT-TAT
TA-TA-TA-TA
PANNG

46
PIII
THE DRAGON BALLS ARE IN THERE!!
UGH !!!
TOONG
WH... WHAT... THE HECK IS HE...
...!!
OWW!! NOW I'M MAD!!
HE'S GOING IN THE TOWER !!!

HE'S ALREADY INSIDE TOWER 8, SIR!!!
AND WE'VE LOST HALF OUR MEN!!
AND YOU HAVE THE GALL TO CALL YOURSELVES THE "WORLD'S MIGHTIEST EVIL ARMY"?!!
BLACK!! WE'RE GOING TO TOWER 8 OURSELVES !!
Y-YES, SIR !!
BOTH OF YOU!!
ON BOARD NOW !!
CAPSULE CORP.

SHEEOO—M
CAPSULE
CAPSULE
DON'T YOU THINK THIS IS A JOB FOR AN *EXPERIENCED* FIGHTER?!
YEAH! I DON'T WANT TO DIE EITHER!
WE'LL NEED EVERY BODY WE CAN GET!!
HASN'T GOKU SAVED EVERY ONE OF YOUR LIVES AT LEAST ONCE?!!
PERHAPS I MIGHT BE OF SOME ASSISTANCE AS WELL...?
...
HEY!! WHAT HAPPENED TO THAT GUY KURIRIN?!
HE WENT SWIMMING OFF TO DO SOME GROCERY SHOPPING. NO BOAT, YOU UNDERSTAND.....

HE'S STRONG ENOUGH TO ACTUALLY DO US SOME GOOD!! WE'VE GOT TO GET HIM TOO!!
HE SHOULD BE RIGHT AROUND HERE SOMEWHERE....
CAPSULE
CAPSULE CORP.

BIP BEEP
PANT PANT

NO ONE... WILL TOUCH...
...THOSE DRAGON BALLS !!
THINGS DON'T LOOK VERY GOOD... THAT SON GOKU IS POWERFUL BEYOND BELIEF...
AND WE ALREADY LOST MOST OF OUR TOP OPERATIVES EVEN *BEFORE* THIS... THANKS TO HIM....

WH-WHAT ?!
THE HEAD-QUARTERS OF THE RED RIBBON ARMY?!
WHAT'S THAT IDIOT THINKING ?!!
HE'S NOT. OBVIOUSLY.
HEH HEH HEH... MY TRIGGER FINGER'S ITCHING...
THIS IS ONE TIME WE REALLY NEED YOU IN YOUR MEAN WARRIOR FORM.... PLEASE DON'T SNEEZE AT A CRUCIAL MOMENT....
PU'AR! HOW MUCH LONGER BEFORE WE ARRIVE ?!
ABOUT.... 40 MINUTES, LORD YAMCHA !!
HY-AH-- !!
RR
FURTHER UP, EH?

HUH ?
THERE AREN'T ANY STAIRS...
YAH !!
B-GOOM
WHOA !!
UGH... !!
I CAN'T STAND IT!! I WILL *NOT* LET THE RED RIBBON ARMY BE DEFEATED BY A BRAT WHO DOESN'T EVEN KNOW WHAT AN ELEVATOR IS!!

Tale 95 • The Fall of Commander Red

PANG
PANG
DOMM
TA
TA
TAT
TAT
TAH
!!
BWAK
KLAM
GOOM

PAPA PA PA
DOMB
BOOOMB!!!
?!
YES !!!
NYAH, NYAH, SERVES YOU RIGHT!!!
YOU CREEPS-- !

WHAT ?!
ULP ?!

YAH-- !!!!

BAMM
AARGH !!!
...
...AIEE... !!

H-HE'S A MONSTER-- !!!!
RUN-- !!!!
ARRRGH !!!
HOW.... PATHETIC!! THEY'RE A DISGRACE TO THE COLOR RED!!
THE REMAINING TROOPS SEEM TO HAVE BEGUN A RETREAT....

G-G-GRR... !!
HE'S JUST A BRAT!!! JUST A STUPID LITTLE BRAT !!!

IT SEEMS WE WERE A BIT TOO LATE IN REALIZING JUST HOW POWERFUL A BRAT....
I'M AFRAID OUR ONLY CHOICE WILL BE TO ABANDON THE BALLS AND RETREAT OURSELVES...

BUT IF THE CHOICE IS THEM... OR YOUR LIFE....?
...
NOW I *REALLY* DON'T WANT TO GIVE UP THOSE BALLS !!
DOMP
GIVE ME A BREAK !!

I WAS SO CLOSE... JUST A LITTLE BIT LONGER.... AND I WOULD HAVE BEEN *TALL*!!
RRRN RRRN
C-CURSE IT...!!

DID YOU SAY... "TALL," SIR?
YOU DON'T MEAN...THAT WE WERE GATHERING THE DRAGON BALLS JUST TO MAKE YOU BIGGER...?

YOU HAVE A PROBLEM WITH THAT?!!
YES !!

WHAT ?!
I THOUGHT WE WERE AFTER WORLD DOMINATION !!!
WE'LL GET TO THAT, WE'LL GET TO THAT !!
BUT A CONQUEROR HAS TO BE CHARISMATIC... DOMINATING... IMPRESSIVE...
I MEAN, WHAT CHICK LOOKS TWICE AT A MIDGET?
...IT WAS FOR SOMETHING AS PETTY AS THAT...
...THAT WE SUFFERED ?!
YOU SEE?!! YOU TALL PEOPLE HAVE NO IDEA HOW WE FEEL!!!
EVER SINCE I WAS A KID...
I'VE BEEN TAUNTED AND RIDICULED... "HEY, HEY, IT'S THAT SHRIMP, RED!"
I'VE EVEN BEEN TOLD "YOU HAVE SUCH A MATURE FACE FOR A LITTLE BOY..."
I HAVE SLAVED AND RISKED MY LIFE FOR ONE REASON ONLY--
TO ADVANCE THE RED RIBBON ARMY'S MISSION OF WORLD CONQUEST!
SHUT UP !!!
I'M THE COMMANDER-IN-CHIEF AND I GET TO SAY WHAT WE DO!!!

DO YOU REALIZE HOW MANY SOLDERS SACRIFICED THEIR LIVES...SO YOU WOULDN'T HAVE TO BE SHORT ?!!
HOW DARE YOU SPEAK TO YOUR COMMANDER LIKE THAT ?!!!
ANYWAY, THEY WOULDN'T HAVE BEEN KILLED IF THEY'D BEEN TRAINED BETTER!!!
PEOPLE SHOULD LEARN TO KEEP THEIR MOUTHS SHUT AND FOLLOW THEIR COMMANDER'S ORDERS!!
!!
BANG

DUB
YOU ARE NOT COMPETENT TO BE COMMANDER.
THE RED RIBBON ARMY WILL REBUILD UNDER NEW COMMAND.
AND COMMANDER BLACK SHALL FULFILL ITS DESTINY.
KRASSH
THEY GOTTA BE RIGHT AROUND HERE.....

SO. YOU'VE FINALLY COME.
ARE YOU THE BOSS?
I AM.
SINCE JUST A MINUTE AGO.
I'M GONNA TAKE THOSE DRAGON BALLS OVER THERE.
FIRST, CONSIDER THIS, SON GOKU.
WHY DON'T YOU AND I GATHER THE DRAGON BALLS TOGETHER?
AND TOGETHER WE WILL RULE THE WORLD.

RULE THE WORLD?
THAT'S RIGHT!
ALL THE POWER OF THE EARTH WILL BE YOURS AND MINE!!

NO WAY! I'M GONNA REVIVE UPA'S DAD WHO GOT KILLED BY ONE OF YOUR GUYS!
...

ALL RIGHT, THEN... WHAT ABOUT THIS?
WHEN WE'VE GATHERED ALL THE DRAGON BALLS, WE CAN BRING BACK TO LIFE THIS FELLOW'S FATHER. THEN YOU WILL JOIN ME IN CONQUERING THE WORLD WITHOUT THE BALLS! TOGETHER WE WILL BE INVINCIBLE!

I TOLD YOU I DON'T WANT TO!!
I DON'T EVEN WANT TO BE ***FRIENDS*** WITH BAD GUYS!!

...I SEE...
THEN THERE'S NO CHOICE LEFT BUT TO BATTLE.
YOU GOT IT!
HEH HEH HEH... YOU ARE FULL OF CONFIDENCE... BUT IT WON'T GO AS EASILY AS BEFORE....
TSWAH !!!
VOOON
HAH !!!
YO !

TAP
TEII
!!!!
FSSHH
DOOB
...GUH...
!!!

NNNGH... !!
HE'S STRONGER... THAN I THOUGHT... !!
JUST GIVE UP!!
GO TO THAT POLICE PLACE !!
KCH
FSS
HUH ?!
POM!
TWA

NEXT: Victory or Defeat??

Tale 96 • The Triumph!

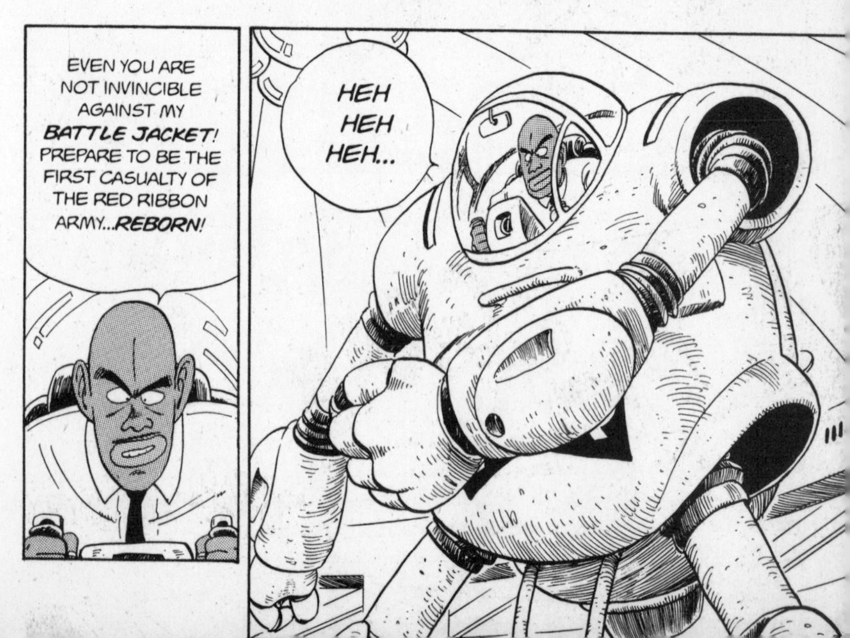

ZAP
SAYO-
NARA
!!
BOOF
WAAH
!!!
GRAB
UNGH
!!!

YOUR TRUE COWARDICE IS EXPOSED!
YEOWW!!
LET-- ME---
GO--!!!
FOOON
EEK!!!
DON'T WORRY, LITTLE BOY-- IT'LL ALL BE OVER IN A SECOND!!!
DWOK
WAAGH!!

DOOOM!
NNNH...
...HENH...
ZAP
RED RIBBON
ZAP
ZAP

BOOM
FWA-HAHA-HAHAHA!! THE BRAT HAS BEEN ERASED OFF THE FACE OF THE EARTH!!
I STAND SUPREME !!
ALL HAIL THE RED RIBBON ARMY!!

I GUESS HE DOESN'T KNOW HOW FAST I AM!
BOING
TSK.
IT'S JUST A SHAME THAT THOSE DRAGON BALLS HE WAS CARRYING WERE DESTROYED ALONG WITH HIM....
TAP
EH ?
HYOH !!
GAH !!!
YOU'RE-- YOU'RE-- !!!
PRETTY COOL, HUH ?
YARGH !!!!

KRIII
...
WHOOPS!
WHAK
...WILL...
DIE...
!!!
...YOU...
HA HA!
YOU'RE
DUMB!

BOMMM
WHOA !!
HYOONNN
DON'T MOVE SO FAST!
TAP
GLANCE
...ALL RIGHT, THEN... !!

PWOK
I HAVE NO CHOICE BUT TO RELEASE THIS MISSILE
AND BLOW YOU TO BITS-- ALONG WITH THIS BASE!!!
WIIIIIN
HEY...
WHAT'S HE TURNING UPSIDE DOWN LIKE THAT FOR?
PII PIII
THIS TIME IS *REALLY* THE END !!!!
KCH

DOOOSH
WHAT.... IN THE.... ?!
SSHHHH
HEY! THAT'S ONE OF THOSE BOMB THINGS !!!!
HYAH !!!!

GONG
HYOOONNN
OWW-- !!!
WH- WHAT ?!!!
Z-GOOOM

SHEESH...
THAT WAS A NICE MOUNTAIN, TOO...
WH-WHAT IS THIS FREAK?!
N-NO ONE'S THAT STRONG...
YOU'LL REGRET THIS !!!
I'LL KILL YOU-- ONE OF THESE DAYS !!!
RED RIBBON
BOMM
HUH?!! IS HE RUNNIN' AWAY ?!
BUT HE'S A BAD GUY....
NNN
...AND I DON'T LET BAD GUYS GET AWAY !!!
NONG

FWAAA
...N-NO WAY...
...IT CAN'T BE... !!
DWOK

TO BE CONTINUED...

DRAGON BALL

TITLE PAGE GALLERY

These chapter title pages were used when these episodes of **Dragon Ball** were originally published in 1986 in Japan in **Weekly Shonen Jump** magazine.

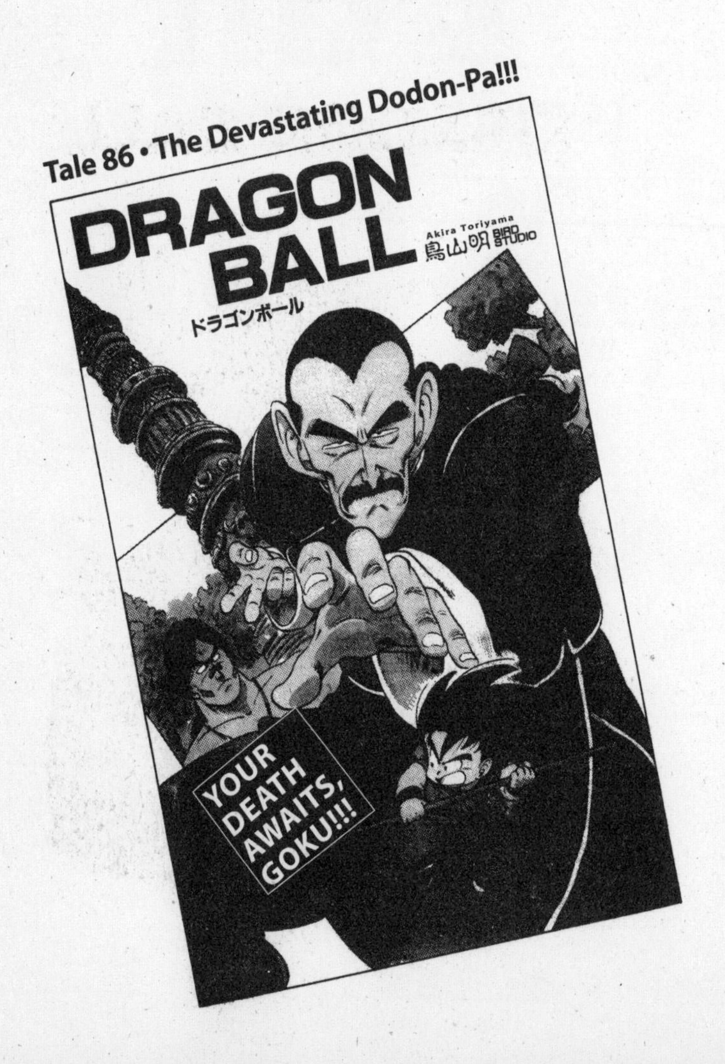

IS THIS THE END...?

Tale 87 • The Great Climb

Akira Toriyama
鳥山明
BIRD STUDIO

Tale 88 • Sage of The Karin Tower

YOU'VE MADE IT
TO THE TOP!
BUT WHO'S WAITING FOR YOU?

Akira Toriyama
鳥山明
BIRD STUDIO

ドラゴンボール
DRAGON BALL
JUST ONE DROP... AND YOU'LL GET STRONGER!
Akira Toriyama
鳥山明
BIRD STUDIO
Tale 89
A Drink of Water

ONCE MORE, THE BIG BATTLE!

Tale 90 • Son Goku Strikes Back!

Akira Toriyama
鳥山明 BIRD STUDIO

DRAGON BALL
ドラゴンボール
Tale 91 • Battle in the Sanctuary!!
WHO
WILL
WIN?
Akira Toriyama
BIRD STUDIO

I'LL BEAT YOU WITH MY BARE HANDS!

Tale 92 • Taopaipai at the Brink

Akira Toriyama
鳥山明
BIRD STUDIO

Tale 93 • Goku's Charge

DRAGON
BALL
Tale 96 • The Triumph!
THERE'S NO
TURNING BACK NOW!!!
RR
Akira Toriyama
鳥山 明
BIRD
STUDIO

SJ
Dr. SLUMP™
Manga series on sale now!
by Akira Toriyama, the creator of Dragon Ball and Dragon Ball Z
When goofy inventor Senbei Norimaki creates a precocious robot named Arale, his masterpiece turns out to be more than he bargained for!
ONLY $7.99
Dr. SLUMP
Toriyama volume 1
On sale at:
www.shonenjump.com
Also available at your local bookstore and comic store.
DR.SLUMP © 1980 by Akira Toriyama/SHUEISHA Inc.
SHONEN JUMP
THE WORLD'S MOST POPULAR MANGA
RATED T FOR TEEN
ratings.viz.com
VIZ media
www.viz.com